Table of Contents

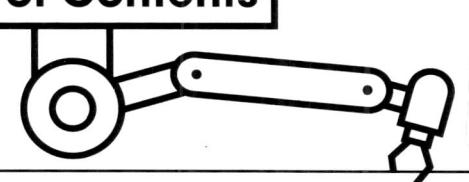

Unit	Week	Grammar	Page
1	1	Common and Proper Nouns	4
	2	Verbs Tenses	6
	3	Common and Proper Nouns; Verb Tenses	10
2	1	Singular and Plural Nouns with Matching Verbs	12
	2	Articles; Demonstratives	14
	3	Articles and Demonstratives; Singular and Plural Nouns with Matching Verbs	16
3	1	Singular and Plural Nouns and Verbs	18
	2	Personal, Possessive, and Indefinite Pronouns	20
	3	Personal Pronouns; Singular and Plural Nouns with Matching Verbs	22
4	1	Adjectives	24
	2	Commas in a Series and in Dates	26
	3	Commas in Dates and Series; Adjectives	28
5	1	Different Kinds of Sentences	30
	2	Prepositions	32
	3	Prepositions; Different Kinds of Sentences	34
6	1	Simple and Compound Sentences	36
	2	Conjunctions; Compound Sentences	38
	3	Conjunctions; Compound Sentences	40
7	1	Possessive Nouns	42
	2	Singular and Plural Nouns with Verbs	44
	3	Singular and Plural Nouns with Verbs; Possessive Nouns	46
8	1	Personal and Possessive Pronouns	48
	2	Present and Past Tense Verbs	50
	3	Past Tense Verbs; Irregular Past Tense Verbs	52
9	1	Expand Simple and Imperative Sentences	54
	2	Adjectives	56
	3	Adjectives; Expand Declarative and Exclamatory Sentences	58
10	1	Expand Declarative and Interrogative Sentences	60
	2	Conjunctions	62
	3	Conjunctions; Expand Declarative and Imperative Sentences	64

Unit	Week	Spelling and Vocabulary	Page
1	1	Short **a** and High-Frequency Words	68
	2	Short **i** and High-Frequency Words	70
	3	Short **o** and High-Frequency Words	72
2	1	Short **e** and High-Frequency Words	74
	2	Short **u** and High-Frequency Words	76
	3	**l**-Blends and High-Frequency Words	78
3	1	**r**-Blends and High-Frequency Words	80
	2	**s**-Blends and High-Frequency Words	82
	3	Final Consonant Blends and High-Frequency Words	84
4	1	Consonant Digraphs **th, sh, ng**	86
	2	Consonant Digraphs **ch, tch, wh**	88
	3	Three-Letter Blends	90
5	1	Long **a** (final **-e**) and High-Frequency Words	92
	2	Long **o** (final **-e**) and High-Frequency Words	94
	3	Soft **c, g,** and High-Frequency Words	96
6	1	Long **i** (final **-e**)	98
	2	Long **e** (final **-e**) and Long **u** (final **-e**)	100
	3	Long **a** Vowel Teams; Long **e** and Long **u**	102
7	1	Long **o** Vowel Teams and Single Letters	104
	2	Long **e** Vowel Teams and Single Letters	106
	3	Long **i** Vowel Teams and Single Letters	108
8	1	/är/ and High-Frequency Words	110
	2	/ôr/ and High-Frequency Words	112
	3	/ür/ and High-Frequency Words	114
9	1	/ou/ and High-Frequency Words	116
	2	/oi/ and High-Frequency Words	118
	3	/o͞o/, /o͝o/, and High-Frequency Words	120
10	1	Silent Letters and High-Frequency Words	122
	2	/ô/ and High-Frequency Words	124
	3	Long **e** Spelled **-y** and **-ey** and High-Frequency Words	126

Introduction

This *Grammar, Spelling & Vocabulary Activity Book* was created to link to the instruction in your *Benchmark Advance Teacher's Resource System* and support each week's grammar and spelling/vocabulary focus. You'll find four practice pages for each week: two for grammar and two for spelling and vocabulary.

The Table of Contents on page 3 lists the target skills for each week and the corresponding practice pages. In addition to providing practice for the targeted instructional goals, many of these pages also provide a spiral review of previously taught skills.

The activities are designed for flexible use in the classroom. Depending on the needs of your students, the activities can be used for guided practice to scaffold students' learning or for independent work, either in class or as homework, to reinforce students' understanding of a skill.

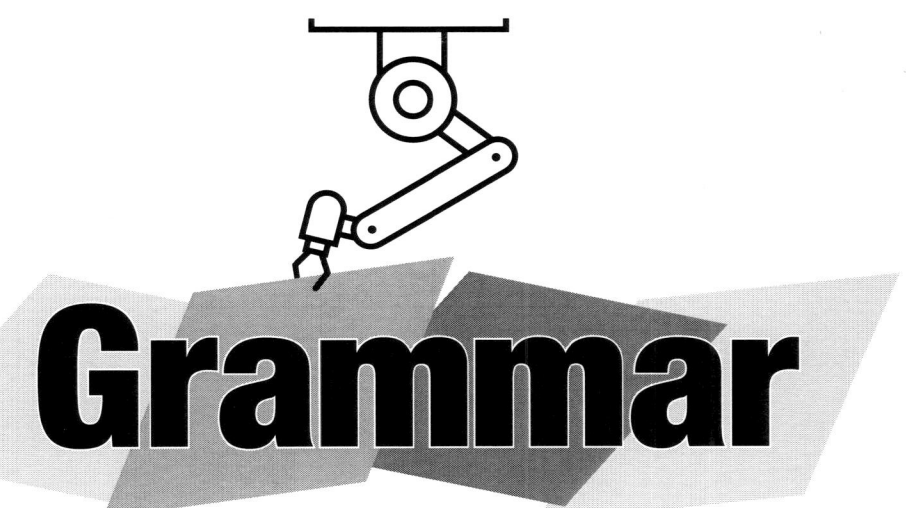

Grammar

Name _____ Date _____

Common and Proper Nouns

A common noun names a person, place, or thing. A proper noun names a specific person, place, or thing. Proper nouns begin with a capital letter.

Common Noun	Proper Noun
friend	Julio
city	Chicago
month	September

Read each sentence. Write the proper noun on the line

1. Mrs. Davila lived near an empty lot. _____

2. Last March, she cleaned it up. _____

3. Her friends on Vista Street helped. _____

4. Arlo weeded. _____

5. Jenna planted seeds. _____

6. By May, the lot had flowers. _____

7. By July, all the flowers had bloomed. _____

8. Saul likes to visit the garden everyday. _____

Common and Proper Nouns

A common noun names a person, place, or thing. A proper noun names a specific person, place, or thing. Proper nouns begin with a capital letter.

Common Noun: The **boy** has two sisters.

Proper Noun: **Kyle** has two sisters.

Circle the proper noun in each sentence. Write it correctly on the line.

1. suzy hopes to make the team. _____

2. He was born in alabama. _____

3. There is a lot of traffic every friday. _____

4. My friend ella is kind. _____

5. The family is moving to chicago. _____

6. The club meets ever tuesday. _____

7. My neighbor is from ohio. _____

8. I don't like the hot weather in florida. _____

Name _____ Date _____

Verb Tenses

> Verbs are words that tell about actions. The tense of a verb shows when the action happens. Past tense verbs tell about an action that already happened. Present tense verbs tell about actions that are happening right now. Future tense verbs tell about actions that will happen at a later time.
>
> **Past:** Last year we **played** soccer.
> **Present:** Now we **play** basketball.
> **Future:** Next year we **will play** baseball.

Read each sentence. Write *present*, *past*, or *future* for the underlined verb.

1. Yesterday, we <u>visited</u> the zoo. _____

2. Tomorrow, Mom <u>will bake</u> cookies. _____

3. Leo <u>respects</u> his teacher. _____

4. We <u>picked</u> up litter in Ward Park. _____

5. The citizens <u>will meet</u> on Monday. _____

Read each sentence. Write the correct form of the verb in parentheses ( ) on the line.

6. Last summer we (travel, traveled) to Mexico. _____

7. Ivan (brushed, brushes) the dog now. _____

Name _____ Date _____

Verb Tenses

The tense of a verb tells when the action happens. To form the past tense of most verbs, add **-ed**. For the present tense, either use the verb as is or add an **-s**. To form the future tense, add **will** in front of the verb.

Past: Yesterday, Ali **walked** to school with Dad.
Present: Today, Ali **walks** with Mom.
Future: Tomorrow, Ali **will walk** with Grandma.

Write the correct form of the verb in ( ) on the line.

1. Next week, we (learned, will learn) about plants.

   _____

2. Last week, we (talk, talked) about animals. _____

3. Rex (fetched, fetches) the ball now. _____

4. Yesterday, Mr. Benson (cook, cooked) vegetables. _____

5. Flowers (will bloom, bloomed) when spring comes.

   _____

Read each sentence. Write *present, past,* or *future* for the underlined verb.

6. After the ride, Jordan <u>stretched</u> her legs. _____

7. I <u>like</u> pizza. _____

Name _____ Date _____

Common and Proper Nouns

A common noun names a person, place, or thing. A proper noun names a specific person, place, or thing. Each main word in a proper noun should begin with a capital letter.

Common Nouns: My **aunt** lives in another **state**.
Proper Nouns: **Aunt Carol** lives in **Michigan**.

Circle the proper noun in each sentence.
Write it correctly on the line.

1. I am visiting france. _____

2. lee created a mural for our hallway. _____

3. My friends live in new york city. _____

4. My whole family eats together on thanksgiving.

_____

5. Summer starts in june. _____

6. mary likes pasta. _____

7. We have a picnic every memorial day.

_____

Verb Tenses

The tense of a verb tells when the action happens. To form the past tense of most verbs, add **-ed**. For the present tense, either use the verb as is or add **-s**. To form the future tense, add **will** in front of the verb.

Past: Last week, Dylan **cooked** dinner.
Present: This week, I **cook** dinner.
Future: Next week, James **will cook** dinner.

Read each sentence. Write *present, past,* or *future* for the underlined verb.

1. Last week, I started a new school. _____

2. I played with some new friends. _____

3. I walk to school every morning. _____

4. Mom will drive me on rainy days. _____

5. I like my new school. _____

Read each sentence. Write the correct form of the verb in parentheses ( ) on the line.

6. Next week, we (painted, will paint) in art. _____

7. Last week, we (molded, will mold) clay. _____

Name _____ Date _____

Singular Nouns with Matching Verbs

A noun names a person, place, or thing. A verb describes an action. A noun is singular if it names only one person, place, or thing. In a sentence, the noun and the verb must match. A singular noun requires a singular verb. Add the letter **s** to a verb when the noun is singular.

Plural: The boys **play** baseball.

Singular: The girl **plays** soccer.

Write the plural version of the verb to match the singular noun.

1. Justin _____ down the sidewalk.
   skip

2. Kyra _____ next to him.
   run

3. A friend _____ them.
   join

4. The sky _____ dark.
   grow

5. Mom _____ everyone inside.
   call

Name _____ Date _____

Plural Nouns with Matching Verbs

A plural noun names more than one person, place, or thing. A plural noun requires a plural verb. To match a plural noun with a plural verb, do not add the letter **s** to the end of the verb.

Singular: Kim **runs** in the park.

Plural: The kids **run** in the park.

Read each sentence. Underline the form of the verb in ( ) that correctly completes each sentence.

1. The cats (chase, chases) the mice.

2. The girls (wash, washes) the dishes.

3. The students (reads, read) the books.

4. The teachers (writes, write) on the board.

5. The skaters (glide, glides) across the ice.

Circle the verb in parentheses ( ) that correctly completes the sentence. Write it on the line.

6. The kittens _____. (nap, naps)

7. The puppies _____. (plays, play)

Name _____ Date _____

Articles

> The words **a**, **an**, and **the** are called articles. Use **the** to tell about an exact person, place, or thing. Use **a** and **an** to tell about any person, place, or thing. Use **a** before a consonant sound and **an** before a vowel sound.
>
> Marco is in **the** kitchen.
>
> He drinks **a** glass of milk.
>
> He eats **an** apple.

Circle the article in the parentheses ( ) that correctly completes the sentence. Write it on the line.

1. I'm at (an, the) zoo! _____

2. I see (a, an) elephant. _____

3. I see (a, an) zebra. _____

4. I pet (a, an) goat. _____

5. I ride on (an, the) red train. _____

6. I want (a, an) apple. _____

7. I wrote (a, an) letter. _____

8. I go to (an, the) store on the corner. _____

Name _____ Date _____

Demonstratives

This, that, these, and **those** are demonstratives.
Demonstratives tell about exact people, places, or things.
This and **that** are used with singular nouns. **These** and **those** are used with plural nouns.

This is my house.

That room is mine.

These toys go in my toy chest.

Those books go on the shelf.

Read each sentence. Underline the correct demonstrative in parentheses ( ) that correctly completes the sentence.

1. (These, This) park is nice.

2. (That, Those) slide is fun.

3. (This, These) swings fly high.

4. (These, That) tree is huge.

5. (Those, That) kids are having a picnic.

Circle the demonstrative in parentheses ( ) that correctly completes the sentence. Write it on the line.

6. (That, Those) boys are playing tag. _____

7. I like to sit on (these, that) big rock. _____

Name _____ Date _____

Articles and Demonstratives

> The words **a**, **an**, and **the** are articles. **This**, **that**, **these**, and **those** are demonstratives. Use articles and demonstratives before nouns.
>
> The pitcher threw **the** ball.
>
> Kim hit **that** ball hard!
>
> She got **a** home run.

Choose the article or demonstrative in ( ) that correctly completes the sentence. Write it on the line.

1. The dog barked at (these, the) mail carrier. _____

2. (These, Those) flowers over there are pretty. _____

3. I will wear (this, those) shirt today. _____

4. Use (this, these) paints for your picture. _____

5. (A, That) girl has purple socks. _____

Read each sentence. Underline the verb in parentheses that correctly completes the sentence.

6. Please put (a, this) coat on the hook.

7. Lila broke (a, an) egg.

Singular and Plural Nouns with Matching Verbs

Singular verbs tell about one person, place, or thing. Add **s** to a singular verb. A plural verb tells about more than one person, place, or thing. Do not add **s** to a plural verb.

Singular: The rabbit **hops.**

Plural: The three rabbits **hop.**

Choose the correct verb. Write it on the line.

1. The spider _____ a web.   (spin, spins)

2. The ants _____ on the log.   (crawl, crawls)

3. The bees _____ near the hive.   (buzz, buzzes)

4. The butterfly _____ its wings.   (spread, spreads)

5. The worms _____ in the dirt.   (dig, dig)

Read each sentence. Underline the verb in the parentheses ( ) that correctly completes the sentence.

6. Grasshoppers (jump, jumps) high.

7. The cricket (chirp, chirps) a song.

Name _____ Date _____

Singular and Plural Nouns

Add **s** to most nouns to make them plural. For nouns ending in **x**, **z**, **s**, **sh**, and **ch**, add **es**. For nouns ending in a consonant and **y**, change the **y** to **i** and add **es**.

one doll	two **dolls**
one ax	three **axes**
one baby	two **babies**

Look at the picture.
Write the noun that goes with the picture.

1. 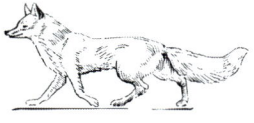 _____

2.  _____

3.  _____

4. 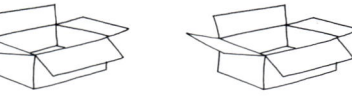 _____

5.  _____

6.  _____

7.  _____

Name _____ Date _____

Singular and Plural Verbs

Add **s** to most verbs to make them singular. Singular verbs tell about one person, place, or thing. For verbs ending in **x**, **z**, **s**, **sh**, and **ch**, add **es**. For verbs ending in a consonant and **y**, change the **y** to **i** and add **es**. Do not add **s** if the sentence tells about more than one person, place, or thing.

The tiger **roars**.	The tigers **roar**.
The girl **fixes** the bike.	The girls **fix** the bike.
The hamster **scurries**.	The hamsters **scurry**.

Read each sentence. Draw a line under the correct verb.

1. Emily and Dad (walk, walks) in the woods.

2. Emily (look, looks) for animals.

3. Birds (sing, sings).

4. A fox (hide, hides) near a tree.

5. Dad (spy, spies) a bug on a twig.

Choose the correct verb. Write it on the line.

6. The sun _____. (set, sets)

7. Dad and Emily _____ home for dinner. (hurry, hurries)

Personal and Possessive Pronouns

Pronouns are words that take the place of nouns. Personal pronouns refer to specific people or things. Possessive pronouns tell who owns something.

Personal	**Possessive**
Carlos rides a bike.	The bike **belongs to Carlos**.
He rides a bike.	The bike is **his**.

Write *he, she,* or *they* for the underlined word or words.

1. <u>Dana</u> gets a basket. _____

2. <u>Paul</u> puts in sandwiches. _____

3. <u>Paul and Dana</u> have a picnic. _____

Write *their, her,* or *his* for the underlined word or words.

4. Dana eats <u>Dana's</u> sandwich. _____

5. Paul sips <u>Paul's</u> water. _____

6. Paul and Dana pick up <u>Paul and Dana's</u> trash. _____

Name _____ Date _____

Indefinite Pronouns

Pronouns are words that take the place of nouns.
Indefinite pronouns don't refer to specific people or things.

Somebody left the lights on.

Nobody is home.

Read each sentence. Circle the indefinite pronoun.

1. Everyone came to the party.

2. Someone is talking.

3. Did you lose something?

4. Nobody liked the movie.

5. Would anyone like to play?

Choose the correct indefinite pronoun. Write it on the line.

6. Did (someone, anything) happen? _____

7. (Nothing, Somebody) is knocking on the door. _____

Personal Pronouns

Pronouns are words that take the place of nouns.

Ming goes to school.

She goes to school.

Write *he*, *she*, *they*, *him*, or *them* for the underlined word or words.

1. Kate lives on a farm. _____

2. Dan milks the cows. _____

3. Kate helps Dan. _____

4. Kate and Dan feed the pigs. _____

5. The pigs like Kate and Dan! _____

6. Kate loves the farm. _____

7. Kate and Dan have many animals. _____

Singular and Plural Nouns with Matching Verbs

Add **s** or **es** to a verb to tell about one person, place, or thing. Do not add **s** or **es** if the sentence tells about more than one person, place, or thing.

The bird **chirps.**

The birds **chirp.**

Read each sentence. Draw a line under the correct verb.

1. The bird (sit, sits) on her nest.

2. Mama Duck (teach, teaches) her ducklings.

3. Five ducklings (swim, swims) in a line.

4. Pam and Jon (throw, throws) bread.

5. The little ducks (eat, eats).

Choose the correct verb. Write it on the line.

6. Papa Duck _____. (watch, watches)

7. He _____ his family safe. (keep, keeps)

8. The baby duck _____ quickly. (learn, learns)

Name _____   Date _____

Adjectives

Adjectives are words that describe nouns. Adjectives tell details about people, places, and things.

The **two big** dogs are **brown**.

Read each sentence. Choose an adjective from the box that best completes the sentence and write it on the line.

| heavy | hot | two | green | tiny |

1. Rosa likes her _____ and red hat.

2. Steve read _____ books.

3. That ant is so _____!

4. Don't touch the _____ oven.

5. Is the box too _____ to lift?

Name _____ Date _____

Adjectives

> Adjectives are words that describe nouns. Adjectives tell details about people, places, and things.
>
> **Six** flowers are in the **tall** vase.

**Read each sentence. Underline the adjective.
Then write the noun it describes on the line.**

1. Arlo likes bright colors. _____

2. Mr. Ruiz read a funny story. _____

3. Julia ate a crunchy apple. _____

4. What's in the large box? _____

5. Fish are quiet pets. _____

6. Mrs. Ellis drives a red car. _____

7. The kitten has soft fur. _____

Name _____ Date _____

Commas in Series

> Use a comma to separate items in a list of three or more items.
> Tina likes apples, bananas, and oranges

Read each sentence. Put commas where they are needed.

1. Fish crabs and sharks live in the ocean.

2. The cow has brown black and tan spots.

3. We can walk run or skip.

Read each sentence. Then rewrite the sentence using the correct punctuation.

4. Ava has blue pink and yellow crayons.

   _____

   _____

5. Jorge can sing dance and act.

   _____

   _____

Name _____ Date _____

Commas in Dates and Series

> Use commas in dates and to separate words in a list.
> Cows, pigs, and ducks live on the farm.
> I had a doctor's appointment on Saturday, April 9, 2016.

Read each sentence. Put commas where they are needed.

1. Bears eat bugs grass and nuts.

2. School started on Monday August 22 2011.

3. You can play hopscotch kickball or tag.

Read each sentence. Then rewrite the sentence using correct punctuation.

4. Grandma was born on May 15 1956.

_____

_____

5. Sam Pat and Kim live next door

_____

_____

Name _____ Date _____

Commas in Dates and Series

> Use commas in dates and to separate words in a list.
> The quilt has blue, red, and yellow patches.
> We moved on Friday, July 31, 2015.

Read each sentence. Put commas where they are needed.

1. The new store opened on Saturday April 2 2016.

2. The store sells toys games and books.

3. It is open on Thursdays Fridays and Saturdays.

Read each sentence. Then rewrite it using the correct punctuation.

4. The sale will start on Friday June 2 2016.

_____

_____

5. Jen Tim and Lee will shop.

_____

6. Camp ends on August 22 2016.

_____

Name _____ Date _____

Adjectives

Adjectives are words that describe nouns. Adjectives tell details about people, places, and things.

Andy ate **four** strawberries.
The **red** strawberries were **delicious**.

Read each sentence. Choose an adjective from the box that best completes the sentence and write it on the line.

| red | cold | one | huge | loud |

1. The _____ music hurt my ears.

2. Elephants are _____ animals.

3. Mom let me have _____ cookie.

4. Jonah has a _____ and blue shirt.

5. Penguins splashed in the _____ water.

Name _____ Date _____

Different Kinds of Sentences

A sentence tells a complete thought and can end in a **.**, **!**, or **?**. Statements or commands end with a period (**.**). Sentences that show a strong feeling end with an exclamation point (**!**). Sentences that ask a question end with a question mark (**?**).

The frog leaped.   Don't move!   Who said that?

Read each sentence.
Write the correct end mark on the line.

1. Dad lifted the box _____

2. The computer beeped _____

3. That cheetah is so fast _____

4. Can you move your toys _____

5. Don't run _____

Rewrite each sentence with the correct end punctuation.

6. What is your favorite color

_____

7. I love that movie

_____

Name _____ Date _____

Different Kinds of Sentences

Sentences can end with a period (**.**), a question mark (**?**), or an exclamation mark (**!**). The end punctuation reveals the type of sentence.

Statement: Maya is seven years old.

Question: Where are you going?

Sentence Showing Excitement: I can't wait!

Read each sentence.
Write the correct end mark on the line.

1. What is your name _____

2. The bike has two wheels _____

3. Be careful _____

4. We tiptoed down the hall _____

5. Who is at the door _____

6. Where are my shoes _____

7. Let's get going _____

8. Are you ready for school _____

9. Leo left his gloves on the bus _____

Name _____ Date _____

Prepositions

> Prepositions connect two words in a sentence and show how they are related. Some prepositions show where something is. Others show when something happens.
>
> Sam put the book **on** the table.
>
> We cheer **during** the game.

Read each sentence. Underline the preposition.

1. We have a tree in our yard.

2. I sit under the tree.

3. Birds perch on the branches.

4. The leaves change color during fall.

5. Then they drop to the ground.

6. I love to run through the leaves.

Write a preposition to complete each sentence.

7. The key is _____ the drawer.

8. I love seeing the branches _____ leaves!

Name _____ Date _____

Prepositions

> Prepositions are words that help connect one word to another word and show how they are related. Some prepositions show where something is. Others show where or when something happens.
>
> I run **around** the block.
>
> We swam **in** the pool.

Choose the preposition in parentheses ( ) that best completes the sentence. Write it on the line.

1. My family is going camping (on, in) Saturday. _____

2. My friend Anna is coming (with, by) me. _____

3. We are sleeping (in, at) tents. _____

4. We will sing songs (by, from) the fire. _____

5. We will toast marshmallows (of, on) sticks. _____

6. It will be fun (for, at) everyone. _____

7. I love being (in, from) nature. _____

8. I will listen to sounds in the woods (around, at) me. _____

Name _____ Date _____

Prepositions

Prepositions are words that help connect one word to another word and show how they are related. Some prepositions show where something is. Others show when something happens.

| at | for | in | on | through |

Choose the preposition from the box that best completes each sentence. Write it on the line.

1. The book is _____ the shelf.

2. School starts _____ 8:30 in the morning.

3. The gift is _____ my teacher.

4. My sister is _____ her room.

5. Jaime walked _____ the door.

6. The bird landed _____ the branch.

7. Eli arrived _____ school first.

8. Lena made a card _____ me.

9. We drove _____ town.

Name _____ Date _____

Different Kinds of Sentences

There are different kinds of sentences. Statements or commands end with a period (.). Sentences that show a strong feeling end with an exclamation mark (!). Sentences that ask a question end with a question mark (?).

I bought shoes.

Soccer is fun!

When is your birthday?

Rewrite each sentence with the correct end mark.

1. What day is it _____

2. I love to dance _____

3. I read two books _____

4. Would you like to play _____

5. You did a great job _____

6. The game is next week _____

7. Where is Julio _____

8. Let's sing _____

Name _____ Date _____

Simple Sentences

A sentence is a group of words that tells a complete thought. All sentences have a noun, or subject, and a verb that describes the action. There are three types of sentences: statements, questions, and expressions of strong feelings. Statements end in a **.**, questions end in a **?**, and sentences that express strong feels and in a **!**.

Statement: The dog barked.
Question: What is your name?
Strong Feelings: That's great!

Read each sentence and write the correct end mark on the line. Choose one of the following: .   ?   !

1. Put your toys away now _____

2. I can't believe it _____

3. The flock flew away _____

4. Where are you going _____

Circle which one is missing, the subject or the verb.

5. Max on the tire.   (subject, verb)

6. Need to buy milk.   (subject, verb)

Name _____ Date _____

Compound Sentences

A compound sentence is made up of two simple sentences that are joined by a comma and a conjunction, such as **and, but, or,** or **so.**

I like dogs, **but** my brother likes cats.
We went to the movies, **and** we got popcorn.

Combine the pair of simple sentences to make a compound sentence. Add a comma and the conjunction in ( ). Write the compound sentence on the line.

1. I want to go. Mom is not ready.   (but)

_____

2. We can walk. We can ride our bikes.   (or)

_____

3. Jon got a book. Then he read it.   (and)

_____

4. It started raining. We went inside.   (so)

_____

5. I want a new book. I have to finish this one.   (but)

_____

Conjunctions

> Conjunctions are used to join two parts of a sentence. Conjunctions include the words **and, but, so,** and **or.** Add a comma before a conjunction when you form a compound sentence.
>
> We can read a book, **or** we can play outside.

Use a comma and a conjunction from the box to combine the sentences. Write the compound sentence on the line.

| and | but | so | or |

1. Alina likes apples. She does not like bananas.

_____

2. The baby cried. His mother picked him up.

_____

3. We will have math. Then we will have recess.

_____

4. Matt will wear his blue shirt. He will wear his black one.

_____

5. I like school. I want to play outside.

_____

Name _____ Date _____

Compound Sentences

> Compound sentences are made up of two simple sentences joined by a comma and a conjunction such as **and, or, so,** or **but**.
>
> We can plant green beans, **or** we can plant tomatoes.
> I would like to play, **but** I have homework to do.

Combine the pair of simple sentences to make a compound sentence. Add a comma and the conjunction in ( ). Write the compound sentence on the line.

1. Roses are pretty. They have thorns.   (but)

   _____

2. Dogs have fur. Turtles have shells.   (and)

   _____

3. We are hungry. We will have a snack.   (so)

   _____

4. Tony will take music. He will take art.   (or)

   _____

5. Anna likes soccer. She likes tennis.   (and)

   _____

Name _____ Date _____

Conjunctions

> Conjunctions are connecting words. They join two parts of a sentence. **Or** and **but** show a difference. **So** and **because** explain why something happens.
>
> Lila can bring her lunch, **or** she can buy it.
> She has money **so** she can buy lunch.

Read each sentence. Choose the conjunction that best completes each sentence. Write the conjunction on the line.

1. Jorge wants to swim, _____ it is too cold.
(but, or)

2. Joan is thirsty _____ it is hot outside.
(and, because)

3. We will go to the museum, _____ we will see art.
(and, but)

4. I missed Grandma, _____ I called her.
(but, so)

5. We can run, _____ we can walk.
(so, or)

Compound Sentences

Compound sentences are made up of two simple sentences joined by a comma and a conjunction such as **and, or, so,** or **but**.

We can find shells, **or** we can build sandcastles.
Cara wants to play, **but** she is sick.

Combine the pair of simple sentences to make a compound sentence. Add a comma and the conjunction in ( ). Write the compound sentence on the line.

1. Carlos speaks Spanish. He is learning French.   (and)

_____

2. We can read. We can draw.   (or)

_____

3. The baby is sleeping. I'm awake.   (but)

_____

4. James likes cereal for breakfast. I like pancakes.   (but)

_____

5. I want to go outside. It is raining.   (but)

_____

Possessive Nouns

Possessive nouns show that a person, place, or thing has or owns something. Add an apostrophe (') and an **s** to turn a singular noun into a possessive noun.
　　the toy of the child
　　the **child's** toy

Replace the underlined words with a possessive.

1. The head of the bird is red. _____

2. The fur of the cat is soft. _____

3. Where is the book of Pam? _____

4. We washed the car of Mom. _____

5. The bed of the dog is new. _____

6. The shoe of Ben is lost. _____

7. The door of the school is open. _____

Name _____ Date _____

Possessive Nouns

> Possessive nouns show that a person, place, or thing has or owns something. Add an apostrophe (') and an **s** to turn a singular noun into a possessive noun.
> The door <u>of the car</u> is open.
> The **car's** door is open.

Write a possessive noun for each sentence.

1. The _____ roar is loud.
    lion

2. I wore my _____ hat.
    brother

3. _____ shirt is blue.
    Sam

4. The _____ blanket is soft.
    baby

5. The _____ bowl is empty.
    cat

6. The _____ fur is brown.
    bear

Singular and Plural Nouns

> Add **s** to a verb to tell about one person, place, or thing. Do not add **s** to the verb if the sentence tells about more than one person, place, or thing.
>
> One **boy runs**.
>
> Two **boys run**.

Choose the correct verb. Write it on the line.

1. The animals _____ for food.   (look, looks)

2. The bear _____ berries.   (find, finds)

3. The squirrel _____ nuts.   (eat, eats)

4. The birds _____ for worms.   (hunt, hunts)

5. Rabbits _____ in the bushes.   (hide, hides)

Choose the correct verb. Write it on the line.

6. Night (fall, falls). _____

7. The creatures (sleep, sleeps). _____

Name _____   Date _____

Singular and Plural Nouns with Verbs

Add **s** to a verb to tell about one person, place, or thing. Do not add **s** to the verb if the sentence tells about more than one person, place, or thing.

One **girl jumps** rope.

Two **girls jump** rope.

Read each sentence. Draw a line under the correct verb.

1. The friends (walk, walks) to the garden.

2. Marta (plant, plants) seeds.

3. Paul (water, waters) the seeds.

4. We (pull, pulls) out weeds.

5. Flowers (grow, grows) in the spring.

Choose the correct verb. Write it on the line.

6. Our parents _____ us plant.   (help, helps)

7. I _____ the garden!   (like, likes)

Name _____ Date _____

Singular and Plural Nouns with Verbs

> Verbs need to be in present tense when we talk about things that are happening now, or in the present.
>
> One **dog barks**.
>
> Two **dogs bark**.

Choose the correct verb. Write it on the line.

1. The family _____ Washington, D.C.   (visit, visits)

2. Lila _____ at the memorial.   (look, looks)

3. The memorial _____ soldiers.   (honor, honors)

4. The boys _____ pictures.   (take, takes)

Read each sentence. Draw a line under the correct verb.

5. Good citizens (follow, follows) rules.

6. Laws (keep, keeps) people safe.

7. The president (lead, leads) the country.

Name _____ Date _____

Possessive Nouns

> Possessive nouns show that a person, place, or thing has or owns something. Add an apostrophe (') and an **s** to turn a singular noun into a possessive **noun**.
>
> the <u>hat of the girl</u>
>
> the **girl's hat**

Write a possessive noun for each sentence.

1. _____ bag is packed.
   Marco

2. _____ basket has sandwiches.
   Mom

3. The _____ rays are hot.
   sun

4. The _____ water is cool.
   pool

5. The _____ fun has begun.
   day

6. The _____ feathers are pretty.
   bird

7. The _____ shirt is colorful.
   boy

Name _____   Date _____

Personal Pronouns

Pronouns are words that take the place of nouns. Personal pronouns are used to avoid repetition of the noun. **I**, **he**, **she**, **we**, and **they** are examples of personal pronouns.

Noun	Personal Pronoun
James has a dog.	**He** has a dog.
James likes his dog.	**He** lines his dog.
Maggie and **Janel** painted a mural.	**They** painted a mural.
Maggie and **Janel** were proud of their work.	**They** were proud of their work.

Choose the personal pronoun from the box that best completes each sentence. Write it on the line.

He	She	I	They	It

1. I live in a house. _____ has a red door.

2. My name is Keisha. _____ am seven years old.

3. Noah lives next door. _____ has a little sister.

4. Sally is Noah's sister. _____ likes to sing.

5. I like to play with Noah and Sally. _____ are my friends.

Name _____ Date _____

Possessive Pronouns

Pronouns take the place of nouns. Possessive pronouns show ownership. **My**, **his**, **her**, **our**, and **their** are examples of possessive pronouns.

    I read **my** book.

    Mrs. Green sat at **her** desk.

Choose the possessive pronoun from the box that best completes each sentence. Write it on the line.

my	his	her	our	their

1. Ella wrote _____ name.

2. Anthony brought _____ flashlight.

3. I packed _____ suitcase.

4. We sat at _____ desks.

5. They ate _____ snacks.

6. I liked _____ snack.

Present Tense Verbs

Present tense verbs tell about actions that are happening right now. When the subject is singular, add **-s** or **-es** to the end of most verbs to make the present tense form. Do not add **-s** when the subject is plural.

Al likes the color purple.

Cara and Raul water the plants.

Write the present tense form of the verb in parentheses ( ) on the line.

1. Zach (play) guitar. _____

2. Marina and Pat (ask) questions. _____

3. Dad (wave) to us. _____

4. The runners (race) around the track. _____

5. Sarah (stir) the soup. _____

6. Mom (drive) us. _____

Name _____ Date _____

Past Tense Verbs

> Past tense verbs tell about actions that already happened. Past tense verbs often end in **-ed**.
>
> He **mailed** a letter.
>
> She **turned** on the computer.

Write the past tense form of the verb in the parentheses ( ) on the line.

1. He (watch) the sky. _____

2. We (learn) about stars. _____

3. Dana (look) at the moon. _____

4. The plants (need) more sun. _____

5. Who (discover) the new planet? _____

6. We (walk) there earlier. _____

7. I (talk) on the phone for an hour. _____

Past Tense Verbs

Past tense verbs tell about actions that already happened. Many past tense verbs end in **-ed**.

   We **landed** safely.

   We **looked** at the stars.

Write the past tense form of the verb on the line.

1. We _____ to school.
   walk

2. Carlos and I _____ outside.
   play

3. I _____ up and down.
   jump

4. Our teacher _____ us inside.
   call

5. We all _____ clean up.
   help

6. I _____ the teacher a question.
   ask

Name _____ Date _____

Irregular Past Tense Verbs

Past tense verbs tell about actions that already happened. Many past tense verbs end in **-ed**, but some do not. These verbs are called irregular verbs. Some examples of irregular verbs include **break/broke, wear/wore, know/knew.**

   Peter **broke** the vase.

   She **wore** a white shirt.

   Kim **knew** the answer.

Underline the verb in each sentence. Then write the past tense form of the verb on the line.

1. I know where to find the keys. _____

2. The movie begin an hour ago. _____

3. Adam know where to find the cat. _____

4. Jack break the chair. _____

5. Lee wear a new jacket. _____

6. I catch the ball. _____

Name _____ Date _____

Expand Simple Sentences

Simple sentences are statements with a single subject and a verb or action word. You can expand simple sentences by adding details or extra information.

I like to read.

I like to read **books about horses**.

Choose a detail from the box to expand each simple sentence. Write it on the line.

a cow	of fresh milk	after milking	a farm	to the barn

1. We visited _____.

2. The farmer took us _____.

3. We milked _____.

4. We washed our hands _____.

5. We got to drink a glass _____.

Name _____ Date _____

Expand Imperative Sentences

Imperative sentences give a command. You can expand imperative sentences by telling how to do something or by describing a noun in the sentence.

Sit at your desk.

Sit **quietly** at your desk.

Choose a detail from the box to expand each imperative sentence. Write it on the line.

for a walk	in the library	before you play	to the teacher	to the shelf

1. Return the book _____.

2. Take the dog _____.

3. Clean your room _____.

4. Do your homework _____.

5. Be nice _____.

Adjectives

Adjectives give information about a noun. Adjectives can describe color, number, size, and kind.

Tina's room has **purple** walls.

Stand next to the **tall** tree.

I prefer **hot** weather.

Underline the adjective in each sentence.

1. Calvin wanted a new toy.

2. He had two choices.

3. He liked the noisy truck.

4. He also liked a talking robot.

5. It was a difficult choice.

6. He decided to save his shiny coins.

7. His mom bought him a large ice cream cone.

8. She bought a small ice cream cone for herself.

Name _____ Date _____

Adjectives

> Adjectives give information about a noun. They can describe color, number, size, and kind.
>
> I have **three** cats.
>
> I have a **big** dog.
>
> I have a **white** bird.

Read each sentence. Write the adjective on the line. Circle the noun it describes.

1. A spider has eight legs. _____

2. The tiny ant carried a crumb. _____

3. The orange butterfly flew by. _____

4. Stay away from the red ants. _____

5. I don't like big bugs. _____

6. I see a fuzzy caterpillar. _____

7. Do not pick the green grass. _____

Name _____ Date _____

Adjectives

> Adjectives give information about a noun. They can describe color, number, size, and kind.
>
> Lou wore **white** shoes.
>
> Jean is a **fast** runner.
>
> Rocco has **three** bags.

Read each sentence. Underline the adjective. Circle the noun it describes.

1. Dad put on his old jeans.

2. He sprinkled tiny seeds around the lawn.

3. He sprayed cool water.

4. The warm sun heated the soil.

5. Soon we had soft grass.

6. Mom dug holes in the brown soil.

7. She planted yellow flowers.

8. Soon there were large blooms.

Name _____ Date _____

Expand Declarative and Exclamatory Sentences

> Declarative sentences make statements. Exclamatory sentences show excitement and end in a **!**. You can add details to expand declarative and exclamatory sentences.
>
> **Declarative:** I am sitting at my desk.
>
> I am sitting **quietly** at my desk.
>
> **Exclamatory:** I can't wait!
>
> I can't wait **to see the movie**!

Expand each declarative or exclamatory sentence with a detail from the box. Write it on the line and add the correct punctuation.

for pie	to pick apples	sweet, red	in my lunch box	with ice cream

1. We are going to the orchard _____

2. I like _____ apples the best _____

3. Mom will use some apples _____

4. I love pie _____

5. I will take an apple _____

Name _____ Date _____

Expand Declarative and Interrogative Sentences

> Compound declarative sentences make a statement and have two complete thoughts. You can expand declarative sentences by adding details and information. Compound interrogative sentences include two complete questions. You can expand interrogative sentences by giving more information about the subject of the question.
>
> We plant vegetables, and we grow flowers.
> We plant vegetables <u>in the garden</u>, and we grow flowers <u>in pots</u>.
> Would you like to go, or would you rather stay?
> Would you like to go <u>to the movies</u>, or would you rather stay <u>home</u>?

Read each sentence. Expand it by adding words or details.

1. We can play _____, or we can read _____.

2. Who makes that _____ shirt, and where can I buy one?

3. We draw _____, or we paint _____.

4. Will you come _____, or will you stay _____?

5. We went _____, and it was fun _____.

Name _____ Date _____

Expand Declarative and Interrogative Sentences

> Compound imperative sentences give two or more commands. You can expand imperative sentences by telling how to do something or describing a noun in the sentence. Compound exclamatory sentences show two complete exclamations.
>
> Tiptoe, and be quiet.
> Tiptoe <u>through the door</u>, and be quiet.
> The ride was scary, but it was fun!
> The <u>fast, spinning ride</u> was scary, but it was fun!

Read each imperative or exclamatory sentence. Expand it by adding words or details.

1. I saw _____, and I ran _____!

2. Listen _____, and don't talk _____.

3. Read _____, and write _____.

4. Let's play _____ because it will be fun!

5. Put on shoes before you go _____.

Name _____ Date _____

Conjunctions

> Use conjunctions such as **and, or, but, so,** or **because** to combine shorter sentences into longer ones.
>
> The tree has green leaves. The tree has pink flowers.
>
> The tree has green leaves **and** pink flowers.

Use the conjunction to combine the sentences.
Write the new sentence on the line.

1. The sky was clear. The sky was blue.   (and)

_____

2. Then the sky got dark. It got cloudy.   (and)

_____

3. We heard thunder. We went inside.   (so)

_____

4. Raindrops fell. The storm did not last long.   (but)

_____

5. We can go to the movies. We can go to the park.   (or)

_____

Name _____ Date _____

Conjunctions

Conjunctions can be used to expand sentences.

I like to ride my bike.

I like to ride my bike **and go swimming**.

Read each sentence. Expand the sentence using the conjunction and a phrase from the box.

fast songs	a horn player	cheered for the band
people could rest	people wanted to dance	

1. The band has a drummer and _____.

2. The band plays slow songs and _____.

3. The band played a fast song because. _____

_____.

4. The band played a slow song so _____.

5. The crowd clapped and _____.

Name _____ Date _____

Conjunctions

> Remember that conjunctions can be used to combine or expand sentences.
>
> I brush my teeth, **and** then I go to bed.
>
> I read a story **and** turn out the lights.

Read each sentence. Underline the conjunction. Write it on the line.

1. It was hot, so I went swimming. _____

2. Is the line straight or crooked? _____

3. Jan likes snow, but she doesn't like rain. _____

4. We went camping and slept in a tent. _____

5. I had a snack because I was hungry. _____

Name _____ Date _____

Expand Declarative and Imperative Sentences

> Declarative sentences make statements. Imperative sentences give commands. You can add details to expand declarative and imperative sentences.
>
> We can make cards, and we can say nice things.
> We can make cards, and we can say nice things <u>to show that we care</u>.
> Eat vegetables and play outside.
> Eat vegetable and play outside <u>to stay healthy</u>.

Add details to expand each compound declarative or imperative sentence.

1. Look both ways, and then cross. _____

2. I dream, so I try. _____

3. Tom bakes, and then he shares. _____

4. Feed the fish and clean their bowl. _____

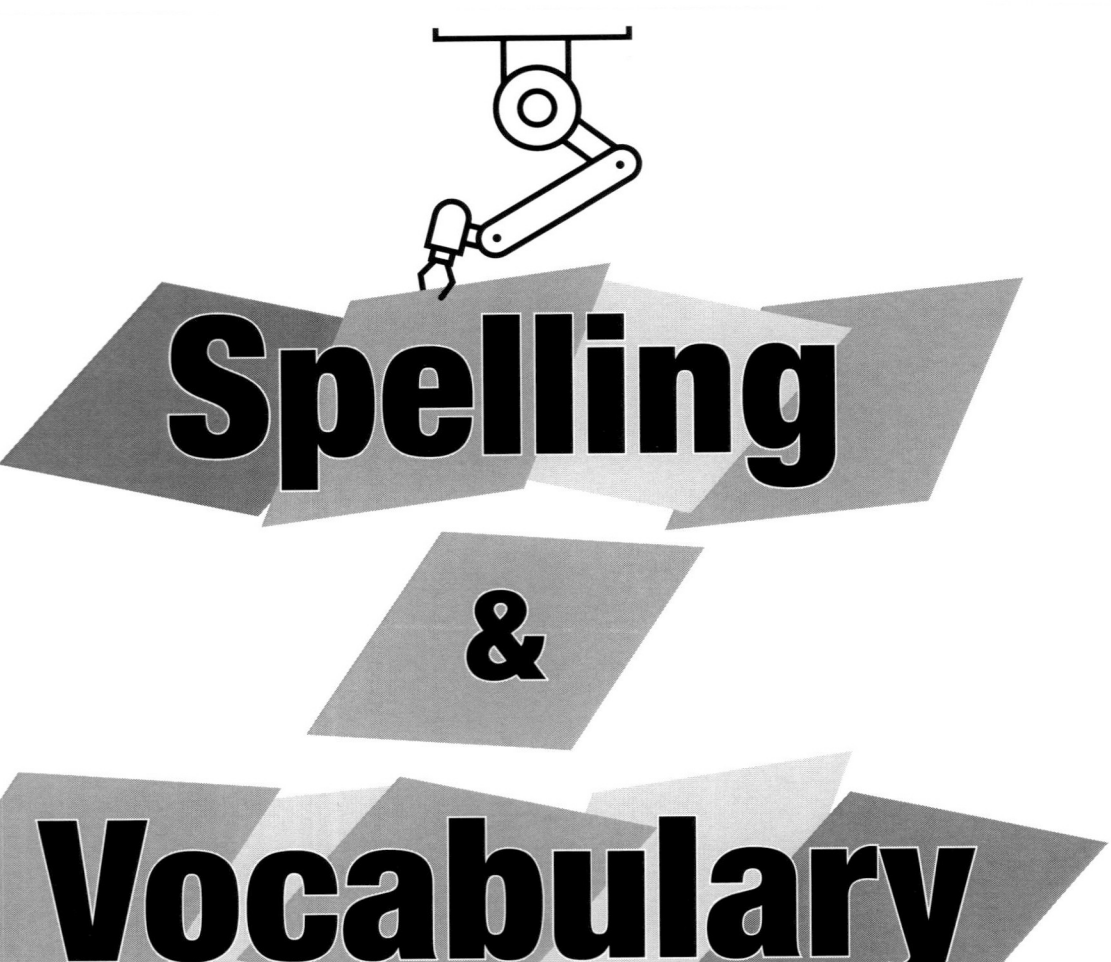

Name _____ Date _____

Short a and High-Frequency Words

| back | cap | had | has | pack |
| pans | ran | sack | see | she |

Write a spelling word for each clue.

1. You wear this on your head. _____

2. It's what you do with your eyes. _____

3. You use these to cook. _____

4. This is a word for a woman. _____

5. It's the opposite of front. _____

6. This is another word for bag. _____

7. This is the past tense of run. _____

8. This is the past tense of have. _____

9. It's what you do to get ready for a trip. _____

Name _____ Date _____

Short a and High-Frequency Words

| back | cap | had | has | pack |
| pans | ran | sack | see | she |

Write the correct spelling words.

Spelling words that end with -ack

1. _____   2. _____

3. _____

4. _____   5. _____

6. _____   7. _____

8. _____   9. _____

10. _____

Name _____ Date _____

Short i and High-Frequency Words

| big | fit | him | hit | kick |
| kids | lid | lips | little | you |

Write a spelling word for each clue.

1. It starts like **fan** and ends like **sit**. _____

2. It starts like **hot** and ends like **pit**. _____

3. It starts like **ball** and ends like **pig**. _____

4. It starts like **lap** and ends like **sips**. _____

5. It starts like **kid** and ends like **sick**. _____

6. It starts like **lab** and ends like **rid**. _____

7. It starts like **kick** and ends like **bids**. _____

8. It starts like **hat** and ends like **Tim**. _____

9. It starts like **lid** and ends like **shuttle**. _____

Name _____ Date _____

Short i and High-Frequency Words

| big | fit | him | hit | kick |
| kids | lid | lips | little | you |

Write the spelling words for the given number of letters.

Spelling words with 3 letters

1. _____   2. _____

3. _____   4. _____

5. _____   6. _____

Spelling words with 4 letters

7. _____   8. _____

9. _____

Spelling word with 6 letters

10. _____

Name _____ Date _____

Short o and High-Frequency Words

| box | cots | doll | hot | jump |
| lock | mop | one | rock | tops |

Circle the spelling word that best completes the sentence. Write it on the line.

1. Please _____ the door.

   box   hot   lock

2. The girls _____ rope.

   jump   mop   doll

3. The fire is _____.

   lock   hot   one

4. The kids sleep on _____.

   rock   tops   cots

5. Jane will _____ the floor.

   mop   rock   jump

6. We play with a _____.

   doll   one   lock

Name _____ Date _____

Short o and High-Frequency Words

| box | cots | doll | hot | jump |
| lock | mop | one | rock | tops |

Write the spelling words for the given number of letters.

Spelling words with 3 letters

1. _____   2. _____

3. _____   4. _____

Spelling words with 4 letters

5. _____   6. _____

7. _____   8. _____

9. _____   10. _____

Circle the two spelling words that rhyme.

11. rock   cot   doll   lock

Name _____ Date _____

Short e and High-Frequency Words

| let | beg | fed | jet | are |
| look | mess | neck | sell | ten |

Read each word below.
Write the spelling word that rhymes with it.

1. pen _____

2. red _____

3. less _____

4. book _____

5. bell _____

6. car _____

7. peck _____

8. egg _____

Write the two spelling words that rhyme with each other.

_____   _____

Name _____ Date _____

Short e and High-Frequency Words

| let | beg | fed | jet | are |
| look | mess | neck | sell | ten |

Write the correct spelling words.

Spelling words that have double letters

1. _____

2. _____

3. _____

Spelling words with 3 letters

4. _____

5. _____

6. _____

7. _____

8. _____

9. _____

Spelling word that ends with -ck

10. _____

Name _____ Date _____

Short u and High-Frequency Words

| cub | duck | here | nut | come |
| cuff | dull | rug | sun | cup |

Write the spelling word that names the picture.

1. _____
2. _____
3. _____
4. _____
5. _____

Read each word below.
Write the spelling word that rhymes with it.

6. rub _____
7. bug _____
8. pup _____
9. cut _____
10. fun _____

Name _____ Date _____

Short u and High-Frequency Words

| cub | duck | here | nut | come |
| cuff | dull | rug | sun | cup |

Write the spelling words for the given spelling pattern.

Spelling words that start with c

1. _____   2. _____

3. _____   4. _____

Spelling words that start with d

5. _____   6. _____

Spelling words that start or end with n

7. _____   8. _____

Spelling words with r

9. _____   10. _____

Name _____ Date _____

l-Blends and High-Frequency Words

| black | class | clock | flat | glad |
| plan | plums | put | slip | what |

Write a spelling word for each clue.

1. This is a color. _____

2. These are a type of fruit. _____

3. This shows the time. _____

4. Use this word to ask a question. _____

5. This is another word for happy. _____

6. You might do this on ice. _____

7. This is your group in school. _____

8. This means to place an object somewhere. _____

9. This is an idea for how to do something. _____

10. The top of a table is this. _____

Name _____ Date _____

l-Blends and High-Frequency Words

| black | class | clock | flat | glad |
| plan | plums | put | slip | what |

Write the spelling words for the given numbers of letters.

Spelling word with 3 letters

1. _____

Spelling words with 4 letters

2. _____   3. _____

4. _____   5. _____

6. _____

Spelling words with 5 letters

7. _____   8. _____

9. _____   10. _____

Name _____ Date _____

r-Blends and High-Frequency Words

| brim | crab | drip | frog | grass |
| now | prop | trim | trip | went |

Write a spelling word for each clue.

1. It starts like **no** and ends like **cow**. _____

2. It starts like **tree** and ends like **sip**. _____

3. It starts like **dry** and ends like **lip**. _____

4. It starts like **crow** and ends like **lab**. _____

5. It starts like **free** and ends like **bog**. _____

6. It starts like **win** and ends like **tent**. _____

7. It starts like **train** and ends like **him**. _____

8. It starts like **bring** and ends like **him**. _____

9. It starts like **prize** and ends like **drop**. _____

Name _____ Date _____

r-Blends and High-Frequency Words

| brim | crab | drip | frog | grass |
| now | prop | trim | trip | went |

Write the spelling words that match each clue.

Spelling words that end with -im

1. _____   2. _____

Spelling words that end with p

3. _____   4. _____

5. _____

Spelling words that have a w

6. _____   7. _____

Spelling words that name animals

8. _____   9. _____

Spelling word that ends with a double letter

10. _____

s-Blends and High-Frequency Words

| out | skin | skip | sled | slip |
| smell | spin | spot | step | was |

Read each word below. Write the spelling word that rhymes with it.

1. bell _____

2. bed _____

3. hot _____

4. shout _____

5. buzz _____

6. pep _____

Write the two spelling words that rhyme with *hip*.

_____   _____

Write the two spelling words that rhyme with *tin*.

_____   _____

Name _____ Date _____

s-Blends and High-Frequency Words

| out | skin | skip | sled | slip |
| smell | spin | spot | step | was |

Write the spelling words for each clue.

Spelling words that start with *sk*

1. _____   2. _____

Spelling words that start with *sl*

3. _____   4. _____

Spelling words with 3 letters

5. _____   6. _____

Spelling words that start with *sp*

7. _____   8. _____

Spelling word that starts with *st*

9. _____

Spelling word that starts with *sm*

10. _____

SPELLING & VOCABULARY   Grammar, Spelling & Vocabulary Activity Book • © Benchmark Education Company, LLC   G1 U3 W2 BLM2

Name _____ Date _____

Final Consonant Blends and High-Frequency Words

| and | best | good | hand | jump |
| nest | pink | trunk | went | who |

Circle the spelling word that completes the sentence. Write it on the line.

1. The elephant has a long _____.

   hand   trunk   nest

2. The bird built a _____.

   nest   jump   pink

3. _____ is my favorite color.

   Who   Good   Pink

4. Hold the cup in your _____.

   hand   trunk   nest

5. We like to _____ rope.

   went   good   jump

84 SPELLING & VOCABULARY

Name _____ Date _____

Final Consonant Blends and High-Frequency Words

| and | best | good | hand | jump |
| nest | pink | trunk | went | who |

Write the spelling words for each clue.

Spelling words that end with *d*

1. _____   2. _____

3. _____

Spelling words that end with *st*

4. _____   5. _____

Spelling words that end with *nk*

6. _____   7. _____

Spelling words that start with *w*

8. _____   9. _____

Spelling word that ends with *p*

10. _____

Name _____ Date _____

Consonant Digraphs th, sh, ng

| bath | bring | our | rang | shop |
| shut | these | thing | this | wish |

Read each word below. Write the spelling word that rhymes with it.

1. fish _____

2. mop _____

3. math _____

4. nut _____

5. sang _____

6. sour _____

7. hiss _____

8. cheese _____

Write the two spelling words that rhyme with each other.

9. _____ _____

Name _____   Date _____

Consonant Digraphs th, sh, ng

| bath | bring | our | rang | shop |
| shut | these | thing | this | wish |

Write the spelling words for the given spelling patterns.

Spelling words with *th*

1. _____   2. _____

3. _____   4. _____

Spelling words with *sh*

5. _____   6. _____

7. _____

Spelling words with an *r*

8. _____   9. _____

10. _____

Name _____ Date _____

Consonant Digraphs ch, tch, wh

| catch | check | chop | hurt | lunch |
| match | much | when | whiff | once |

Write a spelling word for each clue.

1. It starts like **who** and ends like **sniff**. _____

2. It starts like **cheese** and ends like **hop**. _____

3. It starts like **mat** and ends like **such**. _____

4. It starts like **can** and ends like **hatch**. _____

5. It starts like **who** and ends like **pen**. _____

6. It starts like **left** and ends like **bunch**. _____

7. It starts like **cheese** and ends like **deck**. _____

Name _____ Date _____

Consonant Digraphs ch, tch, wh

| catch | check | chop | hurt | lunch |
| match | much | when | whiff | once |

Write the spelling words for each clue.

Spelling words that end with *tch* and rhyme

1. _____   2. _____

Spelling words that start with *ch*

3. _____   4. _____

Spelling words that end with *ch* and do not rhyme

5. _____   6. _____

Spelling words that start with *wh*

7. _____   8. _____

Spelling word that ends with *rt*

9. _____

Spelling word that starts with a vowel

10. _____

Name _____ Date _____

Three-Letter Blends

| because | scratch | scrub | split | sprint |
| squid | squish | strap | stretch | when |

Write a spelling word to complete each sentence.

1. Don't let the cat _____ you.

2. A _____ lives in the ocean.

3. We had to _____ the dirty floor.

4. _____ is your birthday?

5. Theo and Jana _____ the sandwich.

6. I decided to _____ to the finish line.

7. Make sure the _____ on your helmet is tight enough!

8. I took a walk to _____ my back _____ it was hurting.

Name _____ Date _____

Three-Letter Blends

| because | scratch | scrub | split | sprint |
| squid | squish | strap | stretch | when |

Write the spelling words for the given number of letters.

Spelling word with 4 letters

1. _____

Spelling words with 5 letters

2. _____   3. _____

4. _____   5. _____

Spelling words with 6 letters

6. _____   7. _____

Spelling words with 7 letters

8. _____   9. _____

10. _____

Name _____ Date _____

Long a (final -e) and High-Frequency Words

| brave | right | made | plate | came |
| make | skate | take | many | game |

Write a spelling word for each clue.

1. It starts like **man** and ends like **bake**. _____

2. It starts like **sky** and ends like **gate**. _____

3. It starts like **cat** and ends like **name**. _____

4. It starts like **bring** and ends like **save**. _____

5. It starts like **red** and ends like **night**. _____

6. It starts like **girl** and ends like **same**. _____

7. It starts like **man** and ends like **fade**. _____

8. It starts like **tall** and ends like **bake**. _____

Name _____ Date _____

Long a (final -e) and High-Frequency Words

| brave | right | made | plate | came |
| make | skate | take | many | game |

Write the spelling words for the given spelling patterns.

Spelling words that end in *ame*

1. _____   2. _____

Spelling words that end in *ate*

3. _____   4. _____

Spelling words that start with *m*

5. _____   6. _____

7. _____

Spelling words that have an *r*

8. _____   9. _____

Spelling word that starts with *t*

10. _____

Name _____ Date _____

Long o (final -e) and High-Frequency Words

| bone | broke | close | hole | home |
| how | rode | spoke | those | under |

Read each word below. Write the spelling word that rhymes with it.

1. stone _____

2. pole _____

3. now _____

4. dome _____

5. thunder _____

Write the two pairs of spelling words that rhyme with each other.

6. _____   _____

7. _____   _____

Name _____ Date _____

Long o (final -e) and High-Frequency Words

| bone | broke | close | hole | home |
| how | rode | spoke | those | under |

Write the spelling words for the given number of letters.

Spelling word with 3 letters

1. _____

Spelling words with 4 letters

2. _____   3. _____

4. _____   5. _____

Spelling words with 5 letters

6. _____   7. _____

8. _____   9. _____

10. _____

Name _____ Date _____

Soft c, g, and High-Frequency Words

| cent | dance | face | far | gem |
| page | race | stage | strange | try |

Write a spelling word for each clue.

1. It's what a penny is worth. _____

2. It's a long way from somewhere. _____

3. It's a jewel. _____

4. You run in this. _____

5. You do this to music. _____

6. Your eyes, nose, and mouth are part of this. _____

7. A play happens on this. _____

8. This is something weird. _____

9. You turn this when reading a book. _____

10. You attempt to do something. _____

Name _____ Date _____

Soft c, g, and High-Frequency Words

| cent | dance | face | far | gem |
| page | race | stage | strange | try |

Write the spelling words for the given number of letters.

Spelling words with 3 letters

1. _____   2. _____

3. _____

Spelling words with 4 letters

4. _____   5. _____

6. _____   7. _____

Spelling words with 5 letters

8. _____   9. _____

Spelling word with 7 letters

10. _____

Name _____ Date _____

Long i (final -e)

| after | bike | call | line | mine |
| nice | ride | slice | time | white |

Read each word below. Write a spelling word that rhymes with it.

1. kite _____

2. side _____

3. lime _____

4. fall _____

5. like _____

6. nice _____

7. rafter _____

8. mice _____

9. dine _____

Name _____ Date _____

Long i (final -e)

| after | bike | call | line | mine |
| nice | ride | slice | time | white |

Write the correct spelling words.

Spelling words with 4 letters

1. _____ 2. _____

3. _____ 4. _____

5. _____ 6. _____

7. _____

Spelling words with 5 letters

8. _____ 9. _____

10. _____

Name _____ Date _____

Long e (final -e) and Long u (final -e)

| cube | cute | huge | long | mule |
| off | Pete | Steve | these | use |

Write the correct spelling words for each clue.

1. The kitten is _____.
   cube   cute   mule

2. The elephant is _____.
   off   cube   huge

3. _____ a pencil to write your name.
   Use   These   Off

4. Turn _____ the light.
   these   off   long

5. The _____ lives on a farm.
   mule   cube   huge

Choose two spelling words that complete the sentence. Write them on the lines.

6. My friends are named _____ and _____.

100 SPELLING & VOCABULARY

Name _____ Date _____

Long e (final -e) and Long u (final -e)

| cube | cute | huge | long | mule |
| off | Pete | Steve | these | use |

Write the correct spelling words for each clue.

Spelling words with long *u*

1. _____   2. _____

3. _____   4. _____

5. _____

Spelling words that start with an uppercase letter

6. _____   7. _____

Spelling words with an *o*

8. _____   9. _____

Spelling word that starts with *th*

10. _____

Name _____ Date _____

Long a Vowel Teams

| live | mail | paint | pay | rain |
| spray | stay | trail | way | year |

Write the spelling word for each clue. Underline letters that match the vowel team in the spelling word.

1. It starts like **win** and ends like **ray**. _____

2. It starts like **run** and ends like **pain**. _____

3. It starts like **man** and ends like **sail**. _____

4. It starts like **spring** and ends like **way**. _____

5. It starts like **yes** and ends like **fear**. _____

6. It starts like **trip** and ends like **pail**. _____

7. It starts like **stop** and ends like **pay**. _____

Name _____ Date _____

Long e and Long u

| live | mail | paint | pay | rain |
| spray | stay | trail | way | year |

Write the spelling words for the given spelling patterns.

Spelling words with *ai*

1. _____   2. _____

3. _____   4. _____

Spelling words with *ay*

5. _____   6. _____

7. _____   8. _____

Spelling words that do not have a long *a*

9. _____   10. _____

Name _____ Date _____

Long o Vowel Teams and Single Letters

| cold | found | toe | show | flows |
| your | toast | go | soap | hoe |

Read each word below.
Write the spelling word that rhymes with it.

1. hope _____

2. sound _____

3. blows _____

4. roast _____

5. pour _____

6. hold _____

Write the four words that rhyme with each other.

_____   _____

_____   _____

Name _____ Date _____

Long o Vowel Teams and Single Letters

| cold | found | toe | show | flows |
| your | toast | go | soap | hoe |

Write the spelling word that matches each clue.

Long o sound spelled oe

1. _____   2. _____

Long o sound spelled ow

3. _____   4. _____

Long o sound spelled oa

5. _____   6. _____

Long o sound spelled o

7. _____   8. _____

Write the spelling words that do not have long o.

9. _____   10. _____

Name _____ Date _____

Long e Vowel Teams and Single Letters

| brief | people | we | each | field |
| seat | where | need | fleas | wheels |

Write a spelling word for each clue.

1. We play soccer here. _____

2. This word asks a question. _____

3. It's something to sit on. _____

4. There are four on a bus. _____

5. This is a pronoun. _____

6. It's something you must have. _____

7. These are human beings. _____

8. It takes a short of amount of time. _____

9. It refers to every single one. _____

10. These are small insects. _____

Name _____ Date _____

Long e Vowel Teams and Single Letters

| brief | people | we | each | field |
| seat | where | need | fleas | wheels |

Write the correct spelling words.

2 letters

1. _____

4 letters

2. _____   3. _____

4. _____

5 letters

5. _____   6. _____

7. _____   8. _____

6 letters

9. _____   10. _____

Name _____ Date _____

Long i Vowel Teams and Single Letters

| child | find | pies | tie | again |
| bright | country | high | sky | why |

Choose the spelling word from the box that best completes the sentence. Write it on the line.

1. Lee baked two _____.

2. The moon is in the _____.

3. The _____ played with the toy.

4. Can you _____ my keys?

5. Ana wore a _____ pink shirt.

6. The hockey game ended in a _____.

7. _____ is Jenna so sad?

8. Eden will go to camp _____ next year.

Name _____ Date _____

Long i Vowel Teams and Single Letters

| child | find | pies | tie | again |
| bright | country | high | sky | why |

Write the spelling words that match the clue.

Long *i* sound spelled *i*

1. _____ 2. _____

Long *i* sound spelled *igh*

3. _____ 4. _____

Long *i* sound spelled *ie*

5. _____ 6. _____

Long *i* sound spelled *y*

7. _____ 8. _____

Write the spelling words that do not have long *i*.

9. _____ 10. _____

Name _____ Date _____

/är/ and High-Frequency Words

| boy | dark | farm | four | hard |
| park | part | sharp | start | yard |

Write the correct spelling word for each clue.

1. It starts like **pit** and ends like **bark**. _____

2. It starts like **yes** and ends like **card**. _____

3. It starts like **fan** and ends like **harm**. _____

4. It starts like **dip** and ends like **lark**. _____

5. It starts like **pin** and ends like **smart**. _____

6. It starts like **bat** and ends like **toy**. _____

7. It starts like **fill** and ends like **pour**. _____

8. It starts like **hot** and ends like **card**. _____

9. It starts like **shoe** and ends like **harp**. _____

10. It starts like **stop** and ends like **part**. _____

Name _____ Date _____

/är/ and High-Frequency Words

boy	dark	farm	four	hard
park	part	sharp	start	yard

Write the correct spelling words for the given number of letters.

Spelling words with 3 letters

1. _____

Spelling words with 4 letters

2. _____   3. _____

4. _____   5. _____

6. _____   7. _____

8. _____

Spelling words with 5 letters

9. _____   10. _____

Name _____ Date _____

/ôr/ and High-Frequency Words

| born | store | door | move | fork |
| change | thorn | short | soar | more |

Circle the spelling word that completes the sentence. Write it on the line.

1. My hair is cut _____.

   born   short   fork

2. Can I please have _____?

   thorn   move   more

3. Jamal held the _____ open.

   door   soar   change

4. I was _____ in July.

   born   more   fork

5. Tam will _____ next door.

   store   short   move

6. I got new markers from the art _____.

   soar   store   thorn

Name _____ Date _____

/ôr/ and High-Frequency Words

| born | store | door | move | fork |
| change | thorn | short | soar | more |

Write the correct spelling words for each spelling pattern.

Spelling words with *ore*

1. _____ 2. _____

Spelling word with *oor* **Spelling word with *oar***

3. _____ 4. _____

Spelling words with *or*

5. _____ 6. _____

7. _____ 8. _____

Spelling words that do not have the /ôr/ sound

9. _____ 10. _____

Name _____ Date _____

/ûr/ and High-Frequency Words

| bird | clerk | Earth | every | first |
| hurt | nurse | serve | shirt | turn |

Write the correct spelling word for each clue.

1. something you wear _____

2. an animal with wings that builds nests _____

3. a person who works at a medical office _____

4. comes before second _____

5. what you are when you get a cut _____

6. a person who helps you at a store _____

7. the planet we live on _____

8. all things in a group or series _____

9. to bring someone food or drink _____

10. to move and face a different direction _____

Name _____ Date _____

/ûr/ and High-Frequency Words

| bird | clerk | Earth | every | first |
| hurt | nurse | serve | shirt | turn |

Write the correct spelling words for each spelling pattern.

Spelling words with *ir*

1. _____   2. _____

3. _____

Spelling words with *ur*

4. _____   5. _____

6. _____

Spelling words with *er*

7. _____   8. _____

9. _____

Spelling word with *ear*

10. _____

Name _____ Date _____

/ou/ and High-Frequency Words

| before | brown | count | done | down |
| frown | how | loud | round | sprout |

Read each word below.
Write the spelling word that rhymes with it.

1. sound _____

2. cow _____

3. mount _____

4. trout _____

5. cloud _____

6. store _____

7. crown _____

8. town _____

Name _____ Date _____

/ou/ and High-Frequency Words

| before | brown | count | done | down |
| frown | how | loud | round | sprout |

Write the correct spelling words.

Spelling words with *ow*

1. _____   2. _____

3. _____   4. _____

Spelling words with *ou*

5. _____   6. _____

7. _____   8. _____

Spelling words that do not have the /ou/ sound

9. _____   10. _____

Name _____ Date _____

/oi/ and High-Frequency Words

| boy | buy | coin | join | joy |
| moist | point | spoil | toy | walk |

Write the correct spelling word for each clue.

1. has a damp feeling _____

2. a form of money _____

3. a very happy feeling _____

4. something to play with _____

5. to put one foot in front of the other _____

6. to pay money for something _____

7. to rot _____

8. to gesture toward something _____

9. a male child _____

Name _____ Date _____

/oi/ and High-Frequency Words

| boy | buy | coin | join | joy |
| moist | point | spoil | toy | walk |

Write the correct spelling words.

Spelling words with *oy*

1. _____   2. _____

3. _____

Spelling words with *oi*

4. _____   5. _____

6. _____   7. _____

8. _____

Spelling words that do not have the /*oi*/ sound

9. _____   10. _____

SPELLING & VOCABULARY   Grammar, Spelling & Vocabulary Activity Book • © Benchmark Education Company, LLC   G1 U9 W2 BLM2

Name _____ Date _____

/o͞o/, /o͝o/, and High-Frequency Words

| another | bloom | does | good | hook |
| shook | smooth | soon | tooth | wood |

Write the correct spelling word for each clue.

1. It starts like **sad** and ends like **noon**. _____

2. It starts like **hat** and ends like **cook**. _____

3. It starts like **well** and ends like **hood**. _____

4. It starts like **small** and ends like **tooth**. _____

5. It starts like **shed** and ends like **book**. _____

6. It starts like **blend** and ends like **room**. _____

7. It starts like **ant** and ends like **brother**. _____

8. It starts like **goat** and ends like **food**. _____

9. It starts like **dot** and ends like **toes**. _____

10. It starts like **tail** and ends like **booth**. _____

Name _____ Date _____

/oo̅/, /oŏ/, and High-Frequency Words

| another | bloom | does | good | hook |
| shook | smooth | soon | tooth | wood |

Write the spelling words for the given number of letters.

Spelling words with 4 letters

1. _____

2. _____

3. _____

4. _____

5. _____

Spelling words with 5 letters

6. _____

7. _____

8. _____

Spelling words with 6 letters

9. _____

Spelling words with 7 letters

10. _____

Name _____ Date _____

Silent Letters and High-Frequency Words

| better | gnat | knight | knob | know |
| learn | sign | wrap | wrist | wrong |

Read each word below.
Write the spelling word that rhymes with it.

1. right _____

2. song _____

3. fist _____

4. rat _____

5. low _____

6. tap _____

7. nine _____

Name _____ Date _____

Silent Letters and High-Frequency Words

| better | gnat | knight | knob | know |
| learn | sign | wrap | wrist | wrong |

Write the spelling words that have the silent letter pair *gn*.

1. _____   2. _____

Write the spelling words that have the silent letter pair *kn*.

3. _____   4. _____

5. _____

Write the spelling words that have the silent letter pair *wr*.

6. _____   7. _____

8. _____

Write the spelling words that do not have a silent consonant.

9. _____   10. _____

/ô/ and High-Frequency Words

caught	chalk	draw	father	fault
launch	never	small	taught	yawn

Circle the spelling word that completes the sentence. Write it on the line.

1. The teacher wrote with _____.

    draw   chalk   yawn

2. I _____ when I am tired.

    yawn   small   fault

3. The ant is so _____.

    small   chalk   fault

4. I _____ with markers.

    yawn   launch   draw

5. Pam _____ a fish.

    never   short   caught

Name _____ Date _____

/ô/ and High-Frequency Words

| caught | chalk | draw | father | fault |
| launch | never | small | taught | yawn |

Write the spelling words that match the number of letters.

4 letters

1. _____ 2. _____

5 letters

3. _____ 4. _____

5. _____ 6. _____

6 letters

7. _____ 8. _____

9. _____ 10. _____

Name _____ Date _____

Long e Spelled -y and -ey and High-Frequency Words

| blue | chimney | easy | eight | hockey |
| lucky | penny | turkey | valley | windy |

Write the spelling word for each clue.

1. a game you play on ice _____

2. the number after seven _____

3. a color _____

4. a big bird _____

5. one cent _____

6. not hard _____

7. above a fireplace _____

8. narrow area of low land between hills _____

9. having good things happen _____

10. when air is blowing _____

Name _____ Date _____

Long e Spelled -y and -ey and High-Frequency Words

| blue | chimney | easy | eight | hockey |
| lucky | penny | turkey | valley | windy |

Write the spelling words that match the number of letters.

4 letters

1. _____ 2. _____

5 letters

3. _____ 4. _____

5. _____ 6. _____

6 letters

7. _____ 8. _____

9. _____

7 letters

10. _____

SPELLING & VOCABULARY